Chimpanzees

By Sandra Donovan

Steadwell Books

Raintree Steck-Vaughn Publishers

A Harcourt Company

Austin · New York

www.raintreesteckvaughn.com

ANIMALS OF THE RAIN FOREST

Published by Raintree Steck-Vaughn Publishers,
an imprint of Steck-Vaughn Company.

Library of Congress Cataloging-in-Publication Data
ISBN 0-7398-5370-8
Printed and bound in the United States of America
1 2 3 4 5 6 7 8 9 10 WZ 05 04 03 02

Produced by Compass Books

Photo Acknowledgments
Root Resources/Kenneth Fink, 6, 14, 16, 22; Anthony Mercieca, 28–29; Visuals
Unlimited, cover; A.J. Copley, title page, 24; Mark Newman, 8, 21, 26; Chris Crowley,
11, 12; Gerald Corsi, 18.

Editor: Bryon Cahill
Consultant: Sean Dolan

Content Consultant
Cynthia Sims Parr
Animal Diversity Web
University of Michigan Museum of Zoology

This book supports the National Science Standards.

Contents

MOROCCO
TUNISIA
Canary Islands
(SPAIN)
ALGERIA
LIBYA
EGYPT
WESTERN
SAHARA
MAURITANIA
MALI
NIGER
CHAD
SENEGAL
Lake Chad
GAMBIA
GUINEA BISSAU
BURKINA
SUDAN
DJIBOUTI
GUINEA
BENIN
SOMALIA
SIERRA LEONE
IVORY
COAST
TOGO
GHANA
NIGERIA
CENTRAL
AFRICAN REPUBLIC
ETHIOPIA
LIBERIA
Lake Turkana
CAMEROON
EQUATORIAL GUINEA
Lake Albert
UGANDA
KENYA
South Atlantic
GABON
CONGO
ZAIRE
RWANDA
Lake Victoria
BURUNDI
TANZANIA
Lake Tanganyika
MALAWI
Lake Nyasa
ANGOLA
ZAMBIA
Lake Kariba
MOZAMBIQUE
ZIMBABWE
MADAGASCAR
NAMIBIA
BOTSWANA

Range of the
Chimpanzee
Surrounding
Land
Water
Borders
Rivers

SWAZILAND
LESOTHO
SOUTH AFRICA

N
W   E
S

4

A Quick Look at Chimpanzees

What do chimpanzees look like?

Chimpanzees are small apes. Apes do not have tails, but monkeys do. Chimpanzees have short legs and long arms. Their faces are flat and bare. Thick black hair covers most of their bodies.

Where do chimpanzees live?

Chimpanzees live in the forests and rain forests of western and central Africa.

What do chimpanzees eat?

Chimpanzees eat mostly fruit, nuts, and leaves. They sometimes eat meat from other animals, including lizards, birds, monkeys, and small pigs.

This chimpanzee is using its hand to hold its food.

Chimpanzees in the Rain Forest

Chimpanzees are mammals. A mammal is a warm-blooded animal with a backbone. Female mammals give birth to live young and feed them with milk from their bodies. Warm-blooded animals have a body temperature that stays the same, no matter what the temperature is outside.

The scientific name for chimpanzees is *Pan Troglodytes* (PAN TRAH-glow-dite-eez). Pan is the name of a Greek god who was part-man and part-animal. Early travelers to Africa saw wild chimpanzees and thought that this description fit them well.

Chimpanzees belong to the **primate** family, along with monkeys and gorillas. All primates are mammals that have a large brain and hands that can grasp and hold objects.

 These chimpanzees are knuckle walking.

What Do Chimpanzees Look Like?

Chimpanzees are small apes. Male chimpanzees grow up to about 4 feet (1.2 m) tall. They weigh up to 130 pounds (54 kg). Female chimpanzees are smaller. They are about 3 feet (.9 m) tall and weigh less than 100 pounds (45 kg).

Chimpanzees have flat faces. The skin color ranges from pinkish to black depending on the chimpanzee. Young chimpanzees have paler skin, but it becomes darker as they grow older.

A coat of thick, black hair covers most of a chimpanzee's body. No hair grows on the front of their hands and the bottom of their feet. Their ears and faces are usually bare, too. Some older chimpanzees have beards on their chins.

Colored hair shows the age of a chimpanzee. Young chimpanzees have a growth of white hair on the backside that disappears when they grow older. Older chimpanzees may have patches of gray hair on their bodies.

A chimpanzee's arms are much longer than its legs. It uses them to climb trees and swing from branch to branch. They are also useful in reaching fruits that grow on high, thin branches.

Chimpanzees have **opposable** thumbs. The thumb can be placed against the other fingers. The chimpanzee's big toe is opposable, too. This helps chimpanzees hold objects like people do.

Chimpanzees usually walk on their knuckles with the back of their hands touching the ground. This is called knuckle walking. They can also walk upright.

Where Do Chimpanzees Live?

Wild chimpanzees live only in Africa. They are found in 21 different countries from the western coast to as far east as Rwanda and Tanzania.

Most chimpanzees live in forests or rain forests. Rain forests are warm places where many trees and plants grow close together, and a lot of rain falls.

Although most chimpanzees live in rain forests, they can also live in drier **habitats**. A habitat is a place where an animal or plant usually lives. They may live in drier forests and grassland areas. Because chimpanzees eat many kinds of things, they can live in different habitats. Chimpanzees in dry places eat different kinds of plants than the fruits and plants that grow in the rain forests.

Chimpanzees are social animals, which means they live together in groups. A group of between 15 and 120 chimpanzees is called a community. The community is made up of smaller parties of six or fewer chimpanzees. Parties eat, sleep, and travel together. Chimpanzees usually stay with the community in which they were born. But they change parties often throughout their lives.

Many chimpanzees live in and around rain forest trees.

A community has its own home range. This is the space where an animal or group of animals lives most of its life. The size of the home range depends on how many chimpanzees live in the community. Home ranges are usually between 4 and 20 miles (7.4 and 37 km) large. To protect the home range, male chimpanzees will fight chimpanzees from other communities if they try to enter.

▲ This chimpanzee is making a face to show his rank.

Rank

All the chimpanzees in one community know each other. Each chimpanzee has a special rank. A rank is a place in an order from top to bottom, such as first place or second place. All the members of a community know the rank of the other members. Those with higher ranks have more power in the community. They get to mate with the females and eat whatever food they want.

All male chimpanzees are ranked higher than all females. The highest ranking chimpanzee in the community is called the alpha male. The alpha male often puts on a show to remind everyone that he is the boss. He may break off a tree branch and shake it wildly. Then, he may jump around and scream.

Male chimpanzees often fight each other. After a fight, the winner is ranked higher than the loser.

Communication

Chimpanzees can communicate very well with each other. Communicate means to send and receive messages. Chimpanzees communicate with noises and gestures. Gestures are signs made with the hands, face, or body.

Chimpanzees make pant-hoots. A pant-hoot starts with a series of short, soft calls that sound like "ohh" and builds to fast, loud sounds. They also make a special screaming sound that warns other chimpanzees of danger.

Chimpanzees also use a lot of gestures to communicate with each other. They may hold out their hands, turn around, make faces, and even kiss other chimpanzees.

This chimpanzee has used this stick to get honey. It is licking the honey from the stick.

What Chimpanzees Eat

Chimpanzees are **omnivores**. This means they eat both plants and animals. In the rain forest, chimpanzees eat mostly fruits, nuts, seeds, flowers, and leaves. Two of their favorite foods are figs and palm nuts.

Sometimes there is more fruit in the rain forest than usual. This happens because of **mast fruiting**. Mast fruiting is when most of the fruit trees grow fruit at the same time. This happens about every three to seven years. Food is easier for chimpanzees to find at this time.

Chimpanzees also eat other animals. They eat insects, such as ants and termites. Sometimes they eat birds and small mammals they have hunted and killed. They kill animals any way they can. For example, they may squeeze the neck of an animal until it dies.

▲ These chimpanzees are sharing food with each other.

Finding Food

Chimpanzees are among the few animals that make and use tools. A chimpanzee may use rocks to crack open the hard shells of fruit and nuts. When the shells are cracked, they use their fingers to scoop out the soft insides to eat.

Sometimes chimpanzees use tools to catch insects. To make a tool, a chimpanzee pulls all the leaves off a vine or a twig. Then, it places the tool into a termite or ant nest. The insects climb onto it. When the chimpanzee pulls its tool out of the nest, it may have many insects to eat. It uses its lips to suck the insects off the tool. Then, the chimpanzee reuses it to catch more insects. It stops eating when it is no longer hungry.

Parties of chimpanzees move around the rain forest to find food. The leader of the party is a male. He pant-hoots so that other members of the group can follow him as he moves through the rain forest. The group looks for ripe fruit or small animals, such as monkeys, lizards, and pigs. They chase any small animal they see. If they can catch an animal, they will eat it.

Chimpanzees share food with each other. Some scientists believe chimpanzees grunt and bark to let other chimpanzees know they have found food.

Chimpanzees even share food from each other's mouths. Sometimes one chimpanzee may be eating something tasty, such as a bird's egg or a lizard. Then, other chimpanzees signal that they want to share. The first chimpanzee will often open its mouth so that the other chimpanzees can take some food.

This female is looking for a male chimpanzee to mate with.

A Chimpanzee's Life Cycle

Chimpanzees can mate at any time of the year. Females mate only once every four to five years. Males can mate every year if they can find females to mate with.

Females begin mating when they are about 12 years old. Some of their skin turns bright pink so males know that they are ready to mate.

Male chimpanzees can mate when they are about 13 years old. Even so, they usually do not rank high enough to attract females until they are about 15. The male puts on a show to attract a female. He may jump around, move his arms, throw sticks, and scratch the ground.

Sometimes a male and a female chimpanzee leave their party to mate. They may go to the outside of their home range for a few days or for several months.

Young

A female gives birth about eight months after mating. She usually gives birth to one baby at a time. Some females have twins, but this is very rare.

Newborn chimpanzees weigh about 4 pounds (1.8 kg). They are helpless. Their mothers carry them everywhere they go. The mothers feed their babies with milk from their body. This is called **nursing**.

As the chimpanzee grows, it travels with its mother and older brothers and sisters. The father stays in the community, but does not help raise its young. It begins to eat ripe fruit and leaves. When a chimpanzee is about one year old, it starts to play with other young chimpanzees. They tickle, wrestle, and chase each other through the rain forest. By doing this, it learns its rank and how to be a member of the community.

Chimpanzees stop nursing when they are about five years old. Then they begin to search for food with other family members.

This young chimpanzee is patiently licking dirt off its finger.

When young chimpanzees are about eight years old, they enter adolescence. They might leave their mothers to travel with other parties. During this period, they must show respect to older male chimpanzees, or they may be attacked.

By age 15, a chimpanzee is fully grown. It then begins mating and starts a family of its own. Chimpanzees can live to be more than 50 years old.

▲ Chimpanzees in this group are grooming each other.

A Day in the Life of a Chimpanzee

Chimpanzees are part **arboreal** and part **terrestrial**. Arboreal means to live in trees. Terrestrial means to live on the ground. Chimpanzees feed in trees during the day and sleep in trees at night. But they travel around and rest on the ground in the daytime.

Chimpanzees are **diurnal**. This means they are active during the day, and they sleep at night. A chimpanzee wakes up early in the morning. Usually, it begins to look for food right away. It stays in one place only during a gathering. This is when most of the community stays together in one place for up to a few weeks. Gatherings usually happen when there is a lot of one kind of fruit available to eat in one place.

Throughout the day, chimpanzees communicate with members of their party or community. Touching is very important to them. They hug and kiss each other. They also spend a lot of their time grooming each other. To **groom**, they use their fingers to pick or comb through each other's hair. They remove any dirt, insects, and dead skin that they find.

Chimpanzees usually rest in the afternoon. During this time, many older chimpanzees groom each other. Young chimpanzees often play together.

At night, chimpanzees grab leaves and branches and bend them together to make a nest to sleep in. They make a new nest each night.

This chimpanzee is using a loud pant-hoot to communicate.

The Future of Chimpanzees

Scientists think that a chimpanzee's body is more like a human being's than any other animal. Because of this, scientists test medicine on chimpanzees. They are trying to understand diseases and how to cure them in people. Some people think it is good to test medicine on chimpanzees because it might save people's lives. Other people think it is bad because it hurts the chimpanzees or may kill them.

Chimpanzees are also used for entertainment. Entertainment is anything that people do to enjoy themselves. People around the world visit zoos to watch chimpanzees. Chimpanzees even star in movies. Some people think this is good because chimpanzees are so funny. Other people think it is bad because it is not fun for the chimpanzees.

Wild chimpanzees may have problems finding food if the rain forest is destroyed.

What Will Happen to Chimpanzees?

Chimpanzees in Africa are **endangered**. Endangered means something may die out. In 1960, there were 1 million wild chimpanzees. Today, there are less than 250,000. Without help, chimpanzees could soon become extinct. Extinct means there are no more of that kind of animal alive in the world.

People have taught some chimpanzees to use American Sign Language. American Sign Language is a language using hand signals. Chimpanzees use American Sign Language to talk to people and to other chimpanzees.

Chimpanzees are in danger because rain forests are being destroyed. People clear the land for farms and use the wood for buildings. Wildfires also burn large parts of the rain forest. Chimpanzees cannot survive without their habitat.

People also hunt wild chimpanzees in Africa. Some people eat monkeys as food. Others try to catch baby chimpanzees to sell. These hunters often kill the mother chimpanzees. Without adult females to have more babies, there will be fewer baby chimpanzees in the future.

People can help save chimpanzees. Today, many are working to improve the way people in science and entertainment treat chimpanzees. Other people have formed groups that protect wild chimpanzees. In most African countries, it is now against the law to hunt chimpanzees.

flat face
see page 9

opposable thumb
see page 9

opposable big toe
see page 9

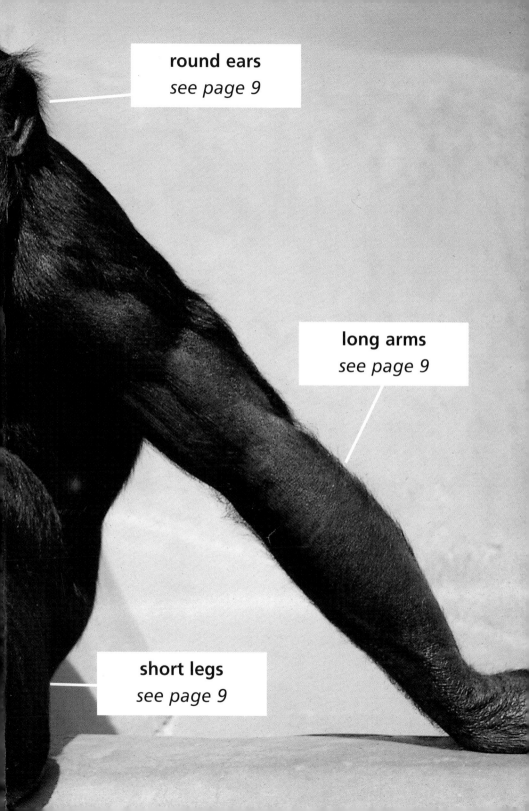

round ears
see page 9

long arms
see page 9

short legs
see page 9

Glossary

arboreal (ahr-BOOR-ee-al)—to live in trees

diurnal (die-UR-nuhl)—most active in the early morning and the early evening

endangered (en-DAYN-jurd)—something that may die out

groom (GROOM)—to clean one's own fur or the fur of another animal

habitats (HAB-i-tats)—places where an animal or plant usually lives

mast fruiting (MAST FROOT-ing)—a time when most of the fruit trees in the rain forest grow fruit at the same time

nursing (NUR-sing)—when a mother feeds her young milk made inside her body

omnivores (AHM-nee-vohrs)—animals that eat both plants and animals

opposable (uh-POH-sa-bul)—the ability of toes or thumbs to grasp and hold objects

primate (PRY-mayt)—a mammal that has a large brain and hands that can grasp and hold objects

terrestrial (tayr-ES-tree-al)—to live on the ground

Internet Sites

Animals of the Rain Forest
www.animalsoftherainforest.org

Jane Goodall Institute
www.janegoodall.org

Useful Address

Save the Chimps
P.O. Box 12220
Fort Pierce, FL 34979

Books to Read

Goodall, Jane. *The Chimpanzee Family Book.*
Saxonville, MA: Picture Book Studio, 1989.

Martin, Patricia. *Chimpanzees.* New York:
Children's Press, 2000.

Index